Social Self-defense

Social Self-defense

Written by Doug Wells

SOCIAL SELF DEFENSE

Written by Doug Wells
Designed and illustrated by Doug Wells

ISBN-13: 978-0983706519
ISBN-10: 0983706514

This book is dedicated to the person who has always inspired me to be the best I can be, challenged be to do better, believed in me no matter what, and has been there for me since the first day I can remember.:

My Grand Mother Rose King.

Today's youth are one of our greatest assets, we must do everything we can to protect them.

Alex Azar

Table of Contents

Introduction

Social self-defense is more of a total picture of self-defense. It encompasses not only the physical act of defending one-self, but also a change in mind where we become aware of our surroundings and thereby create a safe zone, where we are less likely to become a victim. Social self-defense is doing everything possible to AVOID fighting the attacker. Social self-defense is all about using the gray squishy stuff between your ears, and being smarter than the bad guy.

Chapter 1 ▶

What is self-defense

" The act of defending oneself, one's property, or a close relative. "
Merriam-Webster Dictionary

Many times, we think of self-defense as merely defending our self with some form of kicks or punches when attacked. Of course that is probably the most commonly understood form of self-defense. This kind of self-defense is a part of a bigger picture which I am going to call social self-defense.

Social self-defense is more of a total picture of self-defense. It encompasses not only the physical act of defending one-self, but also a change in mind, where we become aware of our surroundings and thereby create a safe zone where we are less likely to become a victim.   Social self-defense is doing everything possible to AVOID fighting the attacker. Social self-defense is all about using the grey squishy stuff between your ears, and being smarter than the bad guy.

Unfortunately, the world in which we live in is increasingly becoming more dangerous, and evil is prevailing. I am sure, at least once someone older than you has said..."when I was a kid we could walk all over town, at any hour and never worry about anything...". I know I have told my children this very thing, but then one day I thought about that and realized, well of course the world was simpler then. We can speculate on what has happened in the world to make it a more dangerous place, and we should, that way, maybe collectively we can make the world a better place for our children and grandchildren. In the meantime we cannot stand idly by and watch as the plots of television shows are played out in real life.

Often times, we put ourselves in a situation that is just right for the predator to take advantage of us. Does that make it our fault, that we became the victim? No, you have the right to be safe at all times. Although this safety is something that should be afforded to all, the predators have learned to take advantage of people when they are most vulnerable. Throughout this book we will discuss places and ways we become vulnerable, how to avoid these, and what we can do to better protect ourselves from the predators in the world.

My intention in this book is not to frighten you, but rather to bring to your mind the fact that monsters are real, they do exist, and they will hurt you if they get the chance. Oh yea, by the way, monsters are human beings who choose to do evil things.

It is well proven, that both males and females, fall victim to the perversities of evil-doers. With that in mind just about everything in this book is interchangeable between the sexes, but I am going to focus more on keeping the girls safe. Statistics show us that predators are more likely to be men preying on women and girls, which makes girls at a higher risk of becoming a victim. Because I am going to talk very straight with you, there will be times in this book where the things I say may be construed as chauvinistic, piggish, racist, and a whole lot of other things, but, I am not. If it helps, you can forgive me now, but it may just save your life, or the life of someone you love. There are some obvious physical differences between men and women, boys and girls, and there are some differences mentally, emotionally, and psychologically between boys and girls, men and women. With that in mind, let us all work together to help keep each other safe. Chivalry is not dead, it is just not being taught any longer.

If you happen to be a fan of the popular television series "Law and Order", you have no doubt seen the disclaimer, "Although inspired in part by a true incident, the following story is fictional and does not depict any actual person or event". That is true, but the events which they depict on the show, really do happen.

We have all seen the television shows and the movies in which the villain takes advantage of the innocent young lady and through a series of events she is now fighting for her life. Hollywood cannot make all of this stuff up, a large percentage of it is true, and that which is made up only acts as a training video for the predators.

I guess, I actually have to say it someplace in this book, I am not in any way advocating vigilantism, the police are your friends. Call them, they are there to help, their number is 911. Program it in your phone. However, I am telling you that you need to take every precaution to keep yourself safe, and hopefully by the end of this book, you will have gained some very helpful information and techniques to do just that.

There are some little tricks, that if we make them a habit in our lives, our safety will increase tremendously. Ok, so here is the deal, I am going to tell you some secrets, and I want you to pass them on to all your friends. Together we can outsmart the bad guys and keep our family and friends safe.

Alright, I am sure you are ready to start, so let's get right to it.

Chapter 2 ➤

Social media

"Evil wants to do evil things."
Joe "Pags" Pagliarulo

With the title of the book being Social Self-defense, I know you are expecting to hear something about social media, and you are right. The very first impression or connection a predator may get with you, is from your Facebook page or the like.

Technology is an incredible thing, it has been given to us in this time, for great things, but just as all good things it can be used for evil as well. Many of us do not truly understand the technology of social networks. Let me give you a simplistic explanation, that hopefully, will help you understand this better.

We have our little Facebook page, where we post fun and interesting pictures, stories and status updates. That information is then uploaded on to a server (a computer). As we know millions of computers connect via this magical network of virtual wires, creating the internet. The information we uploaded on the server, (our Facebook postings) are now being duplicated, backed-up and shared all across the world. So you see, even though we think we are only sharing it with our friends, through the use of modern technology, everything we put on the web is accessible by anyone, anywhere. Oh, and if you think, "ok, I will just delete it". Hate to tell you, that won't work, remember it was duplicated, backed up and shared thousands of times already. With all that said, the best self-defense for this, is not to post it. If you want to post and share with your friends, as the social networks were designed, do so with care. Make sure that the things you post, do not put you or someone else at risk in anyway.

Facebook has been referred to as "internet shopping for burglars". Facebook has some great information on their site, which can help you to protect yourself. This information can be found in the family safety center of Facebook. I have spent a lot of time talking about Facebook, only because it is the most popular social network site at the time this book was being written. Everything I am talking about here, also goes for other social networking sites as well. So, what are some ways that social media can put you at risk.

- pictures

- information

- location

- what we say

Posting pictures is a great way to share with our friends and family, things that are happening in our lives. We went on a family trip one year and chronicled our journey with pictures and postings, which we shared with our family and friends. Even this seemingly innocent virtual trip, put us at risk. As we traveled everyone could see, that we were not at home. This left our home vulnerable to attack. They could tell, we were on the road away from our safety zone and the areas we knew, in foreign places we were unfamiliar with. This left us vulnerable. So, does this mean not to post? That would be your call, I am just saying, that you should be careful what you post and be mindful of the safety factors.

Pictures

When you do post pictures, use some common sense rules.

Only post pictures of yourself and those whom you have permission to post. Do not post pictures of people who have not given you permission to post their image. Do not be afraid to ask someone, odds are they will say it is ok, but, be courteous, and give them the option to say no. Remember it is their safety at risk as well.

Be careful what is in the picture. Do not post pictures where the person is not dressed appropriately, and yes, this includes you as well. A good rule of thumb would be, if you could not wear the clothes to school, then they probably should not be posted on the internet. In case you do not know, predators enjoy looking at pictures of people with little to no clothes on. In fact, they begin to fantasize about the images they see. At that point the person in the picture, becomes simply an object. An object, which the predator desires and sometimes will stop at nothing to get. So, do not be the object of a predators desires.

Every phone has a camera, for that matter many devices have cameras now. Pictures are being taken at an incredible rate these days. Think about this for a moment, how many pictures did you take today? With such ready access to cameras, we are taking pictures of everything we think is cute, funny, sexy, horrible, gross, this list could go on forever. Then of course, we have to share the picture with everyone else, so we post it to the web. This is where we need very careful. Being careful does not only go for what you post, but it goes for what, or who you take pictures of.

Many of the people who are taking and sharing these pictures are children. If you snap a picture of someone, even yourself, with little or no clothes on, you could very well be in possession of child pornography. Yep, that is a crime, and just plain morally wrong. This even goes for some of the "cute", "sexy" poses people do when having their picture taken. Having these pictures on your phone is bad enough, but the second you post, or share them you have committed another horrible crime. See how easy it is to get into trouble, just playing around. Be careful of what and who you take pictures of.

Information

Information, wow that is a huge topic, it literally covers everything about us. Many times, we get caught up in wanting to let all our friends know everything that is going on in our lives. We post our status updates every chance we get. This social media thing is awesome, we can know what people are doing many times before their bestest best friend knows. Oh wait, maybe that is not such a good thing. Think about the damage control, we will have to do if we post something before we tell the person we are posting about. Also remember, just a few minutes ago we talked about how the internet is duplicated, replicated and redundantly backed up. Just in case you missed the English class on the dictionary, redundantly means A LOT. No wonder the law enforcement agencies use social media so much to catch criminals, we are telling the world what we are doing, sometimes before we even do it.

Ok, so what type of information do we need to be careful with? All of it. Let me suggest, that you play the information card a little closer to the vest. Be a bit, NO be a lot more guarded on what information you put out there for the world to see. I am pretty sure that I can look you up on Facebook and gather enough personal information, to do very harmful damage to not only your reputation but also you physically. Wait now, I am not trying to freak you out, maybe scare you a bit, so you understand how important it is, oh ya and I am not a bad guy. Just think, if I can do it, what can the bad guy do?

What kind of information do we need to be careful with? Well, all of it, I will go over a few items, which people tend to be freely giving out without think about the consequences. Some of the most frequently misused information is: Full real names, birthdates, pets names, addresses, place of birth, phone numbers just to name a few. This information is used to establish identity and thus can be used to steal your identity. Do not make your profile public, if you decide to give your information to someone, you can do so privately through a message, email, phone call or better yet, in person.

Location

In this modern age of computers and GPS, it is easier than ever to locate someone. This is especially true, when we advertise where we are going. You have all seen it, maybe you are even guilty of doing it yourself, posting the events and locations you and your friends are going to be at, and what you are going to do tonight. So, now that we have advertised our location to the world, the predator simply, just has to show up. Or better yet, he can get there before us and set a trap for us, which we will fall into because we think nothing can happen to me, that stuff only happens to others. Guess what, you are "others", that stuff happens to everyone, including you. So we show up alone, or with our friends and bam the bad guy strikes and we are on the six o'clock news.

The apps on our phones, Facebook, and many other electronics we use, all have GPS built into them. GPS is very cool. You know, we use a lot of acronyms, and many times we either forget or never understood really that they stand for. Just to help with that, GPS stands for Global Positioning Satellite. That is geek speak for tracking device. Yes that is correct, your phone has a tracking device built into it. This could be a good thing, and I am sure that the intention of having it there was to help people. The problem is, that just like every other thing that is good, evil can use it as well. At least at this time, every device or app has a way of turning off the GPS, or it may be called location. Here is where you need to make some choices. What to turn off and what to leave on. I would suggest, you leave the GPS on in the phone, but limit the access for apps. This way, some apps will be able to use it when you want it, and others will not, depending on the settings. You will need to go through and change the settings and permissions on each app individually, but you will have much more control.

What we say

There is an art that is becoming extinct right before our eyes. That art, is communication. You may not believe this, but not too long ago if you wanted to talk with your friend, you had to get off the couch, walk out the door, walk down the street, up your friends driveway, knock on the door, and ask Mrs. Cleaver if the Beaver could play. Then you would hang out, in person with your friend, and commence in a conversation. Ok dictionary time... a conversation is just like a text message, except that it happens face to face (not facetime). The tools we use in a conversation, are our words, which included the inflection of our voice (pitch, variations and so forth), our eyes, our hands and the entire body. All these aspects of communication are missing in texting, posting, and emailing.

We have all experienced the electronic communication, where we thought someone was joking, but in fact they were serous and mad, but we could not tell for sure, because all we had was the words on the screen. They lacked all the other aspects of communication, which make it effective. You see, "effective communication" is the two way exchange of ideas, in which both parties understand what the other is trying to convey.

We need to be careful what we are saying, this goes for both the social media world as well as our real world conversations. I mean really, no one likes to be insulted, made fun of, or made to look stupid. As humans we tend to be a little more careful with what we say in person. Maybe that has something to do with being a little bit afraid, of the repercussions when making someone mad in real life. When it comes to the virtual world, we all are a lot more brave, and we will tell people what we think without fear of the backlash. We can always delete the email or turn off the computer if we do not like what the other person is saying to us. When you do not have to look someone in the eye and be mean to them it is a lot easier to do it.

A good rule of thumb is, if you would not say it face-to-face to the person, then you probably should not post it either. Your mother probably told you "if you do not have anything nice to say, do not say anything at all". Most of the time this is good advice. Unfortunately, some of the problems we are facing in today's society are a direct result of good people not saying something when things are not right. This makes it a little difficult to not say anything if you cannot say nice things. With a little practice you can say not so nice things in a nice way. You can challenge people and let them know what you believe and how you feel, without causing conflict or war. A lot of times this means we have to choose our words more carefully, and cannot just say the first thing that comes to our minds. Edmund Burke stated "all that is required for evil to prevail is for good men to do nothing". Welcome to 2012, good men have done nothing and evil is prevailing.

Classifieds and Forums

Craigslist is probably the most popular of the classifieds on the internet. Being the most popular makes it a great tool for predators to stalk their prey on. I have to admit, I love craigslist, it is a great tool for selling items, as well as getting great deals. Of course, it is also a virtual playground for criminals.

Let me tell you a little story... Steve has been looking for a motorcycle for some time. He finally found the perfect one on craigslist. This bike met all of his requirements, the price was good and best of all it was not far away. Steve contacted the person selling the bike and arranged to meet him. When Steve arrived at the location he was robbed at gunpoint and beat up. Lucky for Steve all they took from him was his car keys and $500.00, they did not take his life.

Things like this happen all the time. Is this the fault of craigslist? Of course not. It does however remind us that we have to be careful all the time. Just as with everything else you need to use some common sense. Let me give you a few ideas on how you can be a little safer, when buying from classifieds.

- Meet in public places
- Never go alone
- Make sure people know where you are going
- Check things out before you go
  - Google the address
  - View the map – is it in a good part of town
- If it looks or feels wrong, it probably is
- The deal is never so good that you have to take a risk

Chapter 3 ➤

Being aware of your surroundings

> *"Use the environment to your advantage."*

Trust your instincts

It does not matter how well trained you are, how physically fit you are, how smart you are, or even if you are male or female, when you fight back you risk making the situation worse. The bad guy is all amped up on adrenaline and who knows what else, and may become more angry or violent, when they are challenged. The best way to handle this, is to get away.

TIP — Instincts

When the elevator doors open, does that shifty-looking character in the corner make you feel uneasy? Don't get on (or get off if the person is getting on). If you're riding the elevator and you start feeling afraid, get off on a floor where you know you'll find other people. Your safety is all about trusting your instincts.

Trusting your instincts is a great way to avoid a potential attack, before it happens. We all have inside of us, an instinct, intuition, still small voice, Jiminy Cricket, whatever you want to call it, that does not matter. What does matter is, that you trust it. It was put there to help keep you safe, so LISTEN to it.

Here is an example of listening to your instincts. You are running alone, on the school track and you suddenly feel like someone is watching you. That, is the still small voice, telling you to pay attention. Now listen to it, and get back to an area where there are more people around. There is safety in numbers, predators are less likely to attack someone when there are other people around.

Surroundings

Pay attention to your surroundings. When you are walking, or just hanging out, stay in areas which are well lit and open to public view. Staying in areas, where other people are, is always a good idea. Become familiar with the things around you, such as buildings, parking lots, parks, and other places. Be cautious of places people could hide, such as dark corners, bushes, stairways, or behind cars. Even though you may get there faster, avoid shortcuts, that take you through isolated areas, because you may not arrive at your destination.

When you get to your destination, check it out. Scan the room and see who is there, and what they are doing. As you are checking out the location, ask yourself some questions: Does this place look safe? Do I feel comfortable? Do the people here share my ideas of fun activities? If the answers to these questions are no, then you should leave. If you get any feeling, that you are not in the place you should be, or it is not safe, LISTEN to it and leave.

Flight Plan

Before the airplane pilot can even take off, he has to file a flight plan, so that people know where the plane is going and how it will get there, and what time it will arrive. This is something you should also do. It does not have to be as formal, but you should let your friends and family know, what your schedule is for the day. Let them know what classes you have, or sporting events you are going to. If you are going to hang out with friends or whatever you plan to do. I know, it sounds like you are having to check in with your parents again, but, that is not the case. In reality, by letting others know what you are doing, it gives you a safety net, where if by chance you do not show up at a location when you said you would be there, they can check on you.

If your plans change, let someone know. Maybe after the football game, you and some friends decide to go out for ice cream, just call someone and let them know. With someone else knowing your schedule, if something were to happen to you, the search team and police would be able to locate you much faster, and possibly get to you before something extremely bad happens, like you die. So make it a habit to let someone know, where you are going and when you expect to be back.

This should go without saying, but NEVER hitch hike. There was a time and day when this was much safer, but today it is NOT safe at all, so NEVER, EVER hitch hike.

Poise

Whenever you are out, look confident, stand up tall and act as though you know where you are going and are alert and aware of your surroundings. This is a great way to fool the bad guys. You may not be any of those things, you may be scared out of your mind, but if you put on the presence of confidence you will not look like an easy target, and the predators will pass you by.

Carry a cell phone. Your cell phone should be programed with your parents numbers. You could also program the number of someone to contact in the case of an emergency, this could be saved under ICE (In Case of Emergency). That way, if something does happen to you, the police or emergency personnel can contact loved ones and gain valuable information which could save your life.

If you feel uncomfortable, call someone you trust on the phone and talk with them as you are leaving the situation. Many times when the predator sees or hears you on the phone they will leave you alone. When you are on the phone pay attention to things around you, do not zone out and get lost in the conversation.

When you are ridding public transportation, sit near the driver and never fall asleep. Pay attention to the other people on the bus, and keep your distance from those who look shifty. Tell the bus driver where you need to get off, this way he will know to stop and you will not miss your destination.

Make eye contact with people, the predators do not want to be identified. When they know you have seen them, they will move on to someone else who is an easier target. When you see people who just do not look right, do not be afraid to get a good look at them. Do not stare them down, as this could make them angry. Rather make a mental note of what they look like and what they are wearing. If they know they could be identified, they may just move on, but if nothing else, you can let the police know what they look like, if something does happen.

Street

When you are out walking or jogging on the street, be aware of what is going on around you. If you want to listen to music, only have one ear bud in, this way your hearing is not obstructed and you can still hear things that are happening around you. I know, those big headphones are the coolest thing ever and they have great sound, but on the flip side (seventies pop culture reference) they also, make it so you cannot hear what is going on around you. If you cannot hear things around you, you will not be able to hear the predator walking up behind you, and surprise, the bad guy has got you.

I know you learned this years ago, but it seems people forget it, when you are walking on the street or even the side walk, walk on the left side so that you are facing oncoming traffic. The opposite is true when you are on a bike. Bicycles are treated just like cars and are to ride on the right side of the road (not on the sidewalk) and follow all the traffic laws, just like cars.

When you are walking keep your hands out of your pockets, that way you are ready to use them if you are grabbed. If your hands are in your pockets it is too easy for the bad guy to confine you and control you. Walk with confidence, stand tall, keep your eyes and head up, pay attention to what is going on around you. Do not be afraid to look around and even behind you.

When you are walking, some danger signs are: people sitting or standing in odd places, a vehicle which has been driving by several time, a van with no windows, or people who just look out of place. Stay away from these things, and let the police know. They may be doing nothing wrong at all and just enjoying the outdoors like you, but if they look out of place, they are probably not up to anything good, and letting someone know about them, could save your life or the life of someone else.

If you are walking down the sidewalk and the person ahead of you, or coming at you, looks off, cross the street, or change your path. There is always safety in numbers, the more people around, the safer you should be. Use your head, do not walk in dark alleys or shortcuts that take you to places where people are not around.

Chivalry

Ok boys listen up, this is specifically for you, but also applies to the ladies on occasion.

When you drop someone off at their house. Park in a well-lit area, walk them to the door and ensure that they are safely in the house before you leave. For the person being dropped off, after entering the house, leave the outside lights on until your friend has left, and watch from the window to ensure they have left safely.

When you and your friends, get into your cars after an event, do not leave right away. Ensure that everyone is safely in their vehicles, the lights are on and they have started to move. On the other side. Do not get in your vehicle and do other things like fiddle with the radio, put on make-up, etc. start the car, turn on the lights, put the car in gear and drive way.

Environment

Paying attention to your environment could easily save your life. Know how the environment can work for you, or against you. Look around and see what situation you are in. Are you alone, or with friends? Are you up against a wall, or out in the open? What ways could you use to escape? Who is it that you are dealing with? Is the bad guy alone or in a group? What does the person look like, could they be concealing a weapon? Is there anything limiting your abilities? Are you drunk, injured, or trapped? What is around you that could be used as a weapon? Are there people around or are you isolated?

Wow, that is a lot of things to think about, especially if you are in the middle of a scary situation. The trick to this is, to always be doing this. Every moment, of the day, survey the environment and see what is going on. Always be aware of your surroundings and have an exit, a way out, an escape route.

I grew up driving race cars and the biggest rule in racing is to always have an exit. When you are traveling over 100 mile per hour, bumper to bumper with 15 other cars, it only takes one little error to cause a major wreck. Every driver is constantly checking their surroundings and environment to see where they can go if something happens. Because there are so many things that could happen, the drivers have several options in mind, and because things change so fast, so do the options. So, on the race track we would constantly survey our surroundings and make an exit plan, then constantly update that plan as the little things changed.

This is the same in life, there are so many things that could go wrong and they change so fast. We must constantly update our exit plan. If we make it a habit and do this all the time, then it will be second nature. The best thing about second nature, is that it does not take up or energy to think about it, because it just happens.

Time of Day

My father always told me, that nothing good happens late at night. As I was growing up, I challenged that often, thinking, that I was out doing things that were good. My friends and I were watching good movies, playing good games and not causing any trouble. My thinking changed as I grew up, I understood what he was trying to tell me. At night is when all the bad guys come out, they use the cover of darkness to move about and avoid detection. They also use this time to prey on people.

If you have to go out at night, stay in groups. Travel in places that are well-lit and well-traveled by other people. The rule in my family was to be home when the street lights came on. Then if my friends and I wanted to hang out some more, we could do so in the house, where it was safe. I do not think this is such a dated idea, It holds true today as well. Hang out with your friends, but do it in safe places, like your house.

Chapter 4

Home security

"Home Sweet Home"

Our homes should be our safest place, and with a little attention to detail we can make it even safer. Alarms are the number one deterrent for burglars, with dogs being a very close second, if not a tie for first. There are some barking dog alarms on the market, which are motion activated or can be set off by pushing a remote button. These are a good second to having a dog. Even a small dog makes noise and alerts people to the presence of strangers. Big dogs tend to scare criminals more, and for some strange reason, criminals do not like to get bit.

I CAN Make it to the Gate in 2.8 seconds CAN YOU?

Locks

When you first move into a new home, change the locks, you never know who has a key to the house. Keep your house locked and close your blinds. When you blinds are open, especially at night it is very

easy to see into your house and see what you have and who is there or not there. Ensure there is a dead bold on all exterior doors. The lock on the handle is very easy to bypass, a dead bolt is much harder to open without a key.

A lot of times older houses have windows which the locks do not work properly. Take the time to check each window lock and make repairs where needed. The locks that are on the windows are not always the best for security purposes. It is a good idea to add a secondary locking mechanism to each window to ensure they are secure. This could be as easy as a stick preventing the window from sliding.

Hide-a-keys are a great way for us to get into our homes when we lose or forget our keys, but it is also a great way for the criminals to get into our homes as well. Do not hide your house key in a easily accessible place. Even though there are all kinds of cool hide-a-key items sold in the stores, like the fake rock. Do not use them, the criminals have seen these at the store as well and when they see the fake rock by your front door, they will know where the key is. Instead, leave a spare key with a trusted neighbor. If you are one of those people who tend to lock yourself out of the house a lot, you could install a door lock with a combination lock on it. That way, when you are locked out, all you have to do is press the code. Remember the code is just like a key, so do not give it out to people.

Garages are easy entry points to the house. If you have a garage door, install an automatic garage door opener or use dead bolt type locks on both sides of the garage door. Be sure to lock any outside doors to the garage. As well, lock any doors connecting the garage to the house. Keep your garage door closed at all times, that way you are not advertising when you are away from home.

Lighting

Make sure the outside of your home is well-lit. A security light in the driveway, will provide enough light to see people moving around the property. Have security lights by the entrances to your house. Motion lights are a great idea, as they will alert people to movement, and will not run up your electric bill. When placing lights on the exterior of the home, be sure to have lights in places that illuminate the windows and any point of access to the interior of the home. All lights should be facing the house from the street, this way the police and others can see what is going on and are not blinded by lights shining at the street.

What would happen if the lights suddenly went out? Do you know your way around the house when it is pitch black? Do you have flashlights available and handy to get to? For just a few dollars you can purchase a flashlight that plugs into the wall socket, and when the power goes off the flashlight automatically turns on. They make some pretty good small LED flashlights now, get a few of these and leave them throughout your house for easy access when the power goes out.

Neighbors

Get a hold of the neighborhood watch program and become active in keeping your home and your neighborhood safe. Get to know your neighbors. You may not be a people person, but spend a few minutes to get to know your neighbors, they will watch out for you. Let your neighbors know how to get a hold of you if they need to. It is not a bad idea to let the neighbors know your work schedule, this way they will know, if there is activity at your house when you away, they can contact you or the police.

Have a list of neighbors and their phone numbers next to the phone for easy access. Our neighborhood watch captain, created a map with everyone in the neighborhoods house number, names, and phone numbers. This was really great when we moved into the neighborhood, as it helped us to learn the neighbors and gave us a quick reference for phone numbers.

Weapons

There are natural weapons all over your home. Know them and be prepared to use them, if you need to. Every room of your home has some kind of weapon in it. Pens are great weapons, so are sticks, brooms, and of course guns and knives. Just use caution with all weapons, make sure your home is safe for the children as well. I am a firm believer in the second amendment, and believe that every good citizen has the right to have guns and use them to protect themselves, others or their property. If you have guns become a member of the NRA and learn to use, handle and store them safely.

The kitchen and bathrooms are full of weapons, from knives to chemicals. Perfumes and toilet tank lids are all great when you need a weapon on the fly. Laundry rooms have weapons such as and iron, even better when it is hot. The living room has weapons such as pens, channel changers, vases, books and chairs.

Exits

Exit strategy is one of the great secrets of safety, always know your exits from every room of your house. The exits may be a door or a window, be sure to know what is on the other side of that exit. Is it a long drop, a flower bed, or an exit where another bad guy could be waiting? Is there more than one exit from the room, if so know what they are. Are the windows on the second floor of the house above a roof, so when you jump out you land on the roof the of the house. If the upstairs windows have a long drop to the ground, you can get a fire ladder to hang out the window to use as an escape.

Exterior

Do not put your full name on the mail box or in the phone book, this makes it very easy for predators to locate you. On the other side, you do want the police and fire department to find you easily, so have your house number by the door in big numbers, at least 4 inches tall and on the sidewalk where it is easily visible even at night. The house numbers should be visible from 150 feet away. The 911 system will inform the emergency agencies of your address, but they will need to be able to see it in order to quickly find you.

Criminals often times will come to your door, posing as a motorist in distress or a delivery person. Never let strangers into your home. If someone comes and asks to use your phone, make the call for them. If you are home alone, do not open the door for them, ask them to go away, and if you are uncomfortable at the least bit, call the police. It is always better to be safe, than to be a victim.

We all have repair persons come to our homes to work on an appliance, or other things in need of repair. When they get there, ask them for picture identification, and make sure the company logo and information is on the ID. They drove to the house in some sort of vehicle. This vehicle should be clearly marked with the company name. You can always call the company and verify the employee, before letting them into your home. The company should have set an appointment with you, that way will know what time to expect the repair persons.

In this day of electronics, we can let the world know anything and everything very quickly. Never post your schedule for people to see when you will be away from your home or home alone. Don't advertise on your answering machine that you will be gone or on vacation.

Safe room

Create a safe room in your home. This is a place inside your home where you can secure yourself from an attacker. The door to this room should be a solid core or metal door. This room should have a separate phone line, or a cell phone, so you can contact the police. you could also store some food and water in this room and use it as a short term shelter.

Alarm

Having an alarm on your home is a great way to deter criminals. There are many types of alarms, from battery operated wedge alarms to complete monitored alarm systems. Choosing the best for you is a personal choice. Regardless of which you choose, they should all include, an audible alarm that emits a loud noise, a bell or siren. This will scare off on intruders and notify residents or neighbors of an emergency. The alarm should also have a panic button, which you can set off manually. If the system

is monitored, the monitoring agency will notify the police, if not the neighbors will hear the siren and call 911.

Some other quick tips about your home:
- Never open the door without looking first to see who it is.
- Do not give out personal information to people on the phone.
- Use high quality locks
- Use secondary locks on windows
- Use fences and landscape to protect you and your house
- Post all emergency number next to the telephone
- Get a safe
- Report anything suspicious to the police

Chapter 5 ▸━━━━▶

Vehicle security

Many of us feel our vehicles are a safe place, and they can be. On the other hand though, they can be a very dangerous place.

Approach

Before you even enter your vehicle, there are a few simple rule that will help you stay safe and get to your destination without incident. As you approach your vehicle, look around it. Are the tires deflated? Is there debris or class behind or in front of the tires? Is there any fluid leaking underneath. (In the summer there will be some condensation form the air conditioning, which will form a small puddle of water under the engine). If you look for leaks every time you approach your vehicle, you will become aware of what is normal and what is a sign something could be wrong. Are the windows all still in the car. Criminals will knock out windows and steal things from inside the car or even hide in the car waiting for the owner to get into the car. Hiding in the back seat is a very common way of kidnaping people. We get complacent and just go about our business as usual, without thinking that there are bad people in the world and they want to hurt other people. I know you are thinking, kidnappings only happen in the big city, they only happen to famous or rich people. This list could go on, but the truth is, kidnappings happen all the time, to normal everyday people just like you. The only way to prevent it from happening to you, is to pay attention.

Anytime you approach your vehicle and it just does not feel right. Do not keep going, go back to where the people are and ask someone to come out to your car with you. Gentlemen, this is still your responsibility to ensure the ladies get to their car and on their way safely. Walk them to their car, open the door, (of course you already did a visual inspection of the vehicle and the surrounding to make sure it was safe) help the ladies get everything in their car, close the door and wait for them to get on their way. I know that sounded like a chauvinistic statement, no, remember the predator is looking for an easy target. The easy target appears to be the girl or woman by herself, even though she may be very well equipped to defend herself. The target is not so easy when there are two or more people, and the predator is not so ready to take on a guy.

Parking

Park your vehicle at the end of a row where it is more visible. Always park in a well-lit area of the parking lot.

What is parked around your car? Is there another vehicle right next to your car? If so what kind of vehicle? Can you see in that vehicle, or is it a van with the door next to your car. Bad guys will park a van or other vehicle you cannot see into, next to a car and when the owner of the car attempts to get into their car, the bad guy grabs them and takes them into the van.

Paying close attention to what is around your car is an easy way to prevent bad things from happening to you or your loved ones. These things really are not hard, but they do need to become a habit in order for them to work. Because let us face it, it only takes one time for a terrible thing to happen. Keep your guard up and always pay attention.

Before you open your car, look in the windows, both front and back, to ensure that no one is hiding inside your car. When you have verified no-one is in the car, unlock it and get in, then lock it again. Put the key in the ignition, and because you have already checked everything out, drive away.

When parking your vehicle, back it into the parking space. This does a few things, if a thief lifts the hood to hotwire the car they have to do it out in the open, where everyone can see them. By backing into the parking space you are positioning your vehicle for a faster escape if you have to leave quickly.

Parking lots are for cars to hang out in, not people. If you notice people hanging out in the parking lot, or around vehicles, they are probably up to no good. Notify the police of the suspicious activity. If there are suspicious people hanging out in the parking lot, do not go to your vehicle by yourself. Go back to the store, and let the clerks know, so they can have security walk out to your vehicle with you.

Keys

This is a good time to talk about keys. Have your keys ready to open the door was you walk up to your car. If at all possible use the key fob that opens the door. The key fob is the "clicker" that locks and unlocks the cars automatic door locks. (Clicker- that is a pop culture reference to the seventies, when television remote controls actually used a sound to change the channel. The remote control would actually "click". Sorry ADA moment). When you use the key fob, which should be programed to open the driver side door on the first click, all doors on the second click, you will save the time it takes to fumble with the key and unlock the door. This will allow you to enter the car much faster.

Think about that for a moment. I am sure you have seen the movie scene where the victim is fumbling and dropping the keys, as they try to unlock the car. The criminal is right behind them and just as the key enters the lock the criminal grabs the victim and drags them off, beats them or kills them. Once again these things happen, so be prepared and unlock the car as fast as you can, get in and lock the door behind you.

We get busy, we are in a hurry and we stop at the mail box to grab the mail. We leave the vehicle running as we jump out to grab the mail. Just at that moment a quick criminal jumps in the driver's seat and off he goes with the vehicle. It does not matter how long, or short it will take, turn the vehicle off and take the keys out of the ignition.

When the weather is nice, it feels great to drive around with the windows down. When you park the car be sure to roll up the windows and lock the car when you are not next to it. Remember not only is this a valuable piece of machinery, but the criminals will use this tool against you if they get the opportunity. Most crimes involving vehicles are crimes of opportunity. This means that the criminals are wandering around looking for easy opportunities to get into a vehicle.

I have been involved in law enforcement for a long time and one thing I figured out, is that criminals are lazy. Obviously if they were not they would have jobs and not be criminals. Because they are lazy they will take the easy road every time, do not make it easy for them. If they really want to steal your vehicle, or use it to hurt you, make them work for it. Roll your windows up and lock your vehicle.

Hide-a-keys can help us get into our cars when we lock the keys inside, or forget our keys. Do not use hide-a-keys, the criminals know about this little trick and use it to get into your vehicle. Once again do not make it easy for the criminal.

Fuel

There is a little gauge in the instrument cluster on your vehicle. It is kind of funny looking, it has a needle and an E on one side with an F on the other. This is called the fuel gauge, it lets us know how much fuel is in the vehicle. I am going to suggest to you that when the gauge gets to the halfway point, to refill the vehicle. There are a couple of reasons for this. With a full tank of fuel, you can go about 300 miles, that is a long way, you can keep moving and stay ahead of the bad guys. It is also cheaper to fill the tank up if you only have to fill up half the tank. Ok, your right, you fill it up twice as much, so it really is the same amount of money, but it will seem cheaper.

Driving

As you drive be aware of your surroundings, notice if someone is following you. If you are being followed drive to a well-lit public area and ask for help. I am not telling you to use your phone while driving, but if you are being followed, contact the police.

A very common technique used by the bad guys is called a bump and grab. The predator will hit your vehicle, you thinking it was an accident will stop, like you have been taught. You will get out to see if everyone is ok and then deal with the accident. Only, you will find out, that it was not an accident. The predator hit your so you would get out of your car. He now grabs you and can do whatever he wants to you.

Another technique which is very common, is where the predator or an accomplice will lie down in the middle of the road, or place something in the middle of the road, forcing you to stop. They may also be standing by the road flagging you down for help. When you stop they will grab you, and now have control over you to do as they please. If you see someone or something in the middle of the road, or someone flagging you down, do not stop. Go to a well-lit public place and call for help. If you have a cell phone, you can call the police right then. Never get out of your vehicle until the police arrive and it is safe to do so.

Never pick up hitch hikers, and never hitch hike yourself. It does not matter what the gender of the hitch hiker is, Do not pick up hitch hikers. Never let anyone get into your vehicle you do not know.

Break downs

Vehicles are machines, and just like all machines they break down. If your vehicle breaks down on you, pull to safe location. Stay in the vehicle and call for help. Keep the windows rolled up and the doors locked until help arrives. If a stranger stops to help you, tell them, you have called the police for help and they will be their shortly. Do not open the door. Do not get out, until people you can trust arrive to help you.

I know this sounds crazy, but this is the reality of life, and you have to protect yourself. There is a very good chance, the stranger who stopped to help you is just a good Christian, stopping to help. You just cannot afford to take that chance, your life depends on you being smarter than the bad guy. Stay smart, and stay safe.

Chapter 6 ━━▶

De-escalating

"You cannot fight fire with fire"

The bad guys are not always strangers, who jump out at you from a dark alley. Many times, the bad guy who attacks you is someone you have seen before, a school mate, or even someone you know. A great self-defense skill to use is a negotiation tactic called de-escalation.

TIP

VOICE

Draw attention to your situation, shout out words like "Help" or "Police". If you feel threatened other great attention getters are commands like "No!" Or "Get Away!" or "Back Off!"

Remain Calm

De-escalation is simply, speaking or acting in a way that can prevent things from getting worse. Using your words to calm a situation, is a very effective approach to de-escalating a potentially dangerous situation. The trick to calming a situation, is to remain calm. This is not always the easiest thing to do, but try real hard to remain calm on the outside. You can freak out later, after the situation is over.

De-escalation is normally only effective when the bad guy is intimidating you, pushing you, or yelling at you, prior to the situation escalating to physical violence. Being able to use your de-escalation skills at this point, is vital to controlling the situation and giving you a chance to talk your way out of the situation. It also gives you the time to be able to position yourself for a defensive response, if necessary.

Let us talk about some examples of ways to de-escalate, a potentially dangerous situation.

A person comes up to you and starts demanding something from you, you really don't even know what they are wanting because they are yelling so loud and fast, you can hardly make out the words. You can tell they are obviously upset, anxious, and on edge. The worst thing you can do, is to start yelling back at them. This will only raise the level of anxiety and possibly light the fuse for the time bomb already within the person.

Voice

A better approach is, to calmly bring your hands to a position in front of you, about chest level. With your hands open in a non-threatening manner. Closed fists send a signal that you are ready to fight and may very well trigger the other person to fight. In a calm voice and at a lower volume than the other person, ask them a question like. "I'm sorry, I did not hear you, what can I help you with?" Notice the word choice, "I'm sorry" does not challenge the other person, and suggest that you did something wrong, not them. (Of course we know that you did nothing wrong, but in the heat of the moment the other person is not thinking rationally, so we are going to say what we need to in, order to calm the situation.)

"What can I help you with" suggests that you are willing to do something for them, this may be enough to change their thinking pattern, but do not count on it. Also you noticed, that we talked in a clam voice. Which by human nature, people tend to mirror or mimic others in conversation, so hopefully the other person will begin to calm down. Finally, we spoke at a lower volume than the other person, this also will tend to bring their voice level down as well. When a person is not yelling their brain functions a bit more clearly.

De-escalation does not always end the potential attack, but it always helps the situation. By remaining calm and not giving the bad guy any extra ammunition, you maintain some level of control over the situation.

STATS

7% of our communication is "Words".
38% is the "Tone" we use.
55% is our "Body Language"

Body Language

With body language being 55% of our commination, it is very important to understand, how to position our bodies to send the right message. When positioning ourselves against an attacker, we want to both, effectively communicate the proper message and protect our self. All this, while positioning our self for the best defense.

The bad guys want one of three things from you, when they attack you; your valuables (money, cell phone, keys), Your body (beat you, rape you, kidnap you), or your life. It is important to identify what the attacker wants as soon as you can. This will give you the ability to manipulate the situation according to the specific need. Earlier we talked about knowing your surroundings. When you get the bad guy talking, this gives you the chance to be able to examine your surroundings and find ways for the environment to help improve your situation.

Listen

The best skill to use when de-escalating a situation, is to listen. Human psychology tells us that people like to be listened to. When a bad guy attacks you, you get angry. That is natural, so is reacting with violence. A lot of the time, by just listening to the bad guy you will be presented with options to peacefully resolve the situation. Remember God gave you two ears and one mouth, so you can listen twice as much as you speak.

With body language being such a huge part of communication, it is very important to keep the message you are sending with your body and the tone of you speech congruent. Just think of how in-effective it is to say, "I don't want any trouble", when you are standing in a boxers stance with your fists up ready to fight. There is an entire science behind body language and the proper things to do with your body to send the messages you want to send.

For simplicity we are just going to hit on a few basics here. Stand up straight, bring your hands into view with the hands open. This shows the attacker the you are not posing a threat. Do not get too close, on average the three (3) feet of space around a person is their personal space, do not invade it. Lean in just a bit, this will signal the other person you are listening. Do not forget to position yourself for a defense. We will talk more about positioning for a defense in the section on tactics. Do not forget to breath, breath deep and slow, your brain needs oxygen to think clearly, so be sure it get plenty.

In many situations it is important to leave an exit for the attacker. Give them a way to save face and get out of the situation. In the heat of the moment is not the time to play the hero. Defuse the situation, and get to a safe location, then contact the police. Remember the first rule of self-defense is to get away.

Obviously, de-escalation is all situational and does not work every time. I am sure you have heard of the phrase "You cannot fight fire with fire". That is so true when it comes to bag guys. You fight fire with water, so do not throw fuel on the bad guys fire. Anger and confrontation only add to the anger and confrontation the bad guy is already experiencing. Stay calm and be patient, as you deal with the bad guy, this will give you more time to evaluate the situation and decide what to do. Of course there are those times when you have no choice but to react physically to a situation, and those are the times you should rely on the training you have had, to assist you.

Chapter 7 ➤

Personal defense items

*"Better a thousand times careful,
than once dead."*
Ancient Chinese Proverb

There are a multitude of items that can be used as personal defense items. The stores and internet are filled with things you can buy to protect yourself. I am going to list a few of them here, give you a brief idea of how they can be used, but I strongly encourage you to take a self-defense class where you can learn from an expert and practice safely with the item before you carry it. These items are only effective when used properly and safely. Remember they can become weapons for the bad guys very easily, when they take them away from you.

Not all weapons are ones you have to buy at the store, you were born with some of the most effective. The personal self-defense items listed here and other you can purchase, may not be legal in all areas. Be sure to check the laws in your area, as to when and where these items are legal for you to carry and use.

Knees and elbows

Your knees and elbows can inflict great damage and cause intense pain to an attacker. Your knees and elbows are comprised of large hard bones which are attached to large powerful muscle groups. These are great to use when stuck in close quarters with the bad guy. They also do not require any special training to use. You already know how to hit with these tools, because you have been using them all your life. Now there are some ways you can use them, which are more effective and a self-defense trainer can show you how to do this. But, for the most part the gross motor skills of bringing the knee to the groin works great.

Breathing

You may not think of breathing as a weapon, but it really is. Actually, it is part of a weapon. The weapon is your body. Your body needs oxygen to operate, if you do not breath, you do not get oxygen, and your body (the weapon) does not work.

Breath in deep and slow. This will allow for good oxygen disbursement. Now that you have breathed in, you have to exhale. If you exhale quickly at the same time you punch or kick you will help to increase your power, making your kicks and punches stronger.

Voice

Your voice is one of the best weapons you have. You can control people simply by saying things. By yelling "stop" people will stop. By yelling "help" people will come and help. When you are in a dangerous situation, you need to be loud and clear. Yell as loud as you can, and repeat yourself.

Make sure people around you know what is going on. Sometimes, this is as simple as yelling. Give commands, yell out loud, make sure people can hear you. Do not worry about how you sound, that does not matter, just make a lot of noise and be loud about it.

Pen

A pen can be used to jab into someone's eye, or press very hard into the soft area under the jaw. You can jab it into the chest or just about any area of the body you can make contact with, and it will hurt very bad.

Keys

We all carry keys, these can be a very effective weapon and you can always have them at the ready. Put your keys on a little bit bigger ring, so there is enough room for your keys and a finger to go through the ring. When you carry your keys put one finger through the ring, place a key between each finger, so they are poking out of your fist.

If you have a kubaton, have it resting so it points out the back of your hand, away from your thumb. With your keys in this position you can walk very naturally and it does not appear that you are ready to fight someone. Although you now have a weapon that is at the ready, by simply tightening your fist. The keys can be used to rake across the bad guys face, or stab at their throat. If the kubaton is there it can be quickly accessed to inflict severe pain and damage to the attacker.

Kubaton

A kubaton is a piece of metal about 6-7 inches long, with a key ring on one side and a point on the other. They usually have some decorative designs on them, making them pleasing to look at. The kubaton is a good defensive tool as, most people carry keys with them everywhere. Holding the kubaton in your fist, with the point sticking out away from your thumb, allows you to use it to inflict great pain. That is the trick, this device is designed to inflict pain. You can hit someone in the chest, shoulders, arms, legs, eyes, anywhere you can strike them. Remember, at this point the only rule is staying alive. The attacker started it, and if you stop you lose, and if you lose, you could die.

Pepper spray

Pepper spray or mace are both effective. They both do just about the same thing, they burn the eyes and irritate the sinuses. when they do this, they make it difficult for the attacker to continue with the attack, giving you time to get away.

They are very simple to use, simply point the spray at the attacker and give one second burst of spray directly into the eyes of the attacker. If you point it at yourself, it will do the same to you as it does to the attacker, so be sure to point it in the right direction.

Tasers

Tasers and stun guns come in a variety of styles and sizes. They are actually pretty simple to operate. You simply push the button, activating the device and touch it to the attacker. The device generates somewhere around 4.5 million volts of electricity, which will stop an attacker.

Some of the devices have flashlights on them, others even have a siren built into them to help you attract help. Once the attacker is incapacitated, get away and call police. Just as with all personal self-defense items, if you lose the item to the attacker, it can now be used on you.

Knife

Knives are great tools, they can be used for all kinds of things. They come in as many designs and styles as you can think of. When choosing a knife, keep in mind what you are intending to use it for. With that information a knife dealer can help you to decide which is best for you.

Knives can be used to cut, stab, and slice. The problem with a knife is that you have to be close to use it, and the bad guy probably has one to. Anyone can buy a knife, but not everyone knows how to use one properly. I highly recommend that if you are going to carry a knife for protection, you take a class on how to use it properly.

There are some very specific laws concerning knives. Be sure to check with the local law enforcement agency to find out what sizes and types of knives are legal to carry in your area.

Gun

The Second Amendment of the United States Constitution states: ***"A well regulated militia, being necessary to the security of a free state, the right of the people to keep and bear arms, shall not be infringed."*** I believe in this as well as all of the Constitution, and you should as well. You should do everything you can to uphold this Constitution and help to ensure a free America.

When it comes to protecting ourselves, sometimes the last resort is to use a gun. Remember guns don't kill people, people kill people. Guns are simply a tool, just like a thousand other tools that can and are used to kill people.

A gun is a tool which can be used to protect yourself, others and your property. If you choose to use this tool, use it wisely and with caution. They are not toys, you can hurt someone very badly with them, and even kill them.

NEVER carry a gun without proper training and the ability to be able to use the gun safely and properly. Take a defensive handgun course and learn the proper use of a gun. Take a concealed handgun course and carry a gun responsibly. Join the NRA and support gun rights.

I have but one rule to tell you about guns. If you point a gun at someone you better be prepared to pull the trigger. Because they are!

Chapter 8 ➤

Physically stop the threat

"When it comes to self-defense losing is not an option.."

Throughout this book, we have discussed alternative options to actually engaging the attacker. Let me first state here, that it is always the best policy to avoid the situation, or to remove yourself from the situation if at all possible. Yes, that includes running away if you can. You do not have to be the big bad person and fight your way out, unless that is the only option left.

TIP DOG

If you have a dog, take it with you when you are walking alone. Even little dogs bark and snarl enough to cause a potential attacker to think twice.

Because we live in a world that is increasingly becoming more dangerous, as the population of the towns and cities rises, the economy fluctuates, and general chaos runs wild, there will always be bad guys. Villains have been here since the Earth was created, remember Lucifer in the Garden of Eden, yep evil-doers have been here since time began and will continue until Christ comes again. Therefore, knowing that simple fact, you have a choice to make, you can just go about your life and see where it takes you and accept the things that happen to you. Or, you can prepare yourself in in event that you are confronted with a threatening situation.

Remember, I said fighting is bad, but I am drawn to a statement my father told me as I was growing up. "Never start a fight, but if you cannot avoid it, do not lose." his intention, was not to tell me this so that I became a bully. Rather he wanted to make sure, that I was prepared to defend myself, if the need arose. Now, my dad was a Marine, so we have to translate the phrase into average Joe language. This is what he really was trying to tell me. Be a peace maker, do not go out looking for trouble, do your best to stay clear of situation where trouble hangs out. In the event that trouble finds you and you are not able to talk your way out of the situation or avoid a confrontation, then you will need to use the physical skills of self-defense in order to protect yourself. When it comes to self-defense losing is not an option. The biggest reason losing is not an option, is because many times, losing means dying. I don't know about you, but I am not going to let some ignorant person take away my liberty, freedom, and definitely not my life.

So how do we protect ourselves? We have been discussing several ways thus far to avoid the situation, to de-escalate a threatening situation, and to get away if at all possible, but sometimes, all that is not enough and the last resort, did you get that, THE LAST RESORT is to physically stop the threat.

My daughter enjoys watching scary movies. Typically in these movies there is a bad guy of some sort chasing a young girl. Often during the chase he will catch up to her and try to attack her. She will kick, bite, throw things, hit the bad guy, and use various other tactics to get way. For the suspense factor, she will many times knock the bad guy out, hurt him some way, or stun him just enough so she can run away again. Then what happens, yes, he gets up and chases her again, and then he catches her, tortures her, rapes her or kills her. I hate to tell you this, but Hollywood did not invent this script, it happens every day in the real world. This exact scene is played out in somebodies life every day.

The big question is, how do we avoid being the victim? The answer is, being prepared. How do we get prepared for such an evil as this? We learn, we train, and we be mindful of our surroundings.

I have been involved in law enforcement quite literally my entire life, and the one constant I have found that helps people be prepared for threatening situations is Martial Arts. No, you cannot go rent Kung Fu Panda or The Karate Kid and be prepared. Do you have to study Martial Arts for years, in order to be prepared? No. There are some very effective techniques you can learn in minutes, to help you to defend yourself. Do not get me wrong, studying Martial Arts would be a great opportunity to learn not only the techniques you can use to defend yourself, but also gain discipline and confidence, become more physically fit, and live a healthier life.

If you are interested in learning techniques that can save your life or the life of someone you love, then you will need to do a little research. There thousands of people out there who teach some form of Martial Arts, Self-defense class or the like. The problem is for every good instructor there are at least two bad instructors. So, now you are asking, How do I find a good instructor? The answer may not be as simple as looking in the phone book. You will need to spend some time and effort to find someone to teach you. Go and visit the studio of the instructor, talk with the instructor and staff. You should feel comfortable not only in the building, but also with the instructor and staff. Every studio, staff members and instructors have differences in their philosophies and the manner in which they teach. Find the instructor and studio that most closely matches your own personal philosophies. This way you will feel better about them and you will desire to learn more, you will even stay involved longer and enjoy it more.

There are a lot of styles and options out there. I have found, that if you can find an Martial Arts Academy you may do better. The word Academy is the important part. This means that the studio is teaching a multitude of techniques or blended techniques and is more concerned about your learning, than if you learn a specific discipline or not. The reason is these types of places tend to teach the philosophy of the Art, and may even mix disciplines in an effort to better serve the students, while still maintaining the integrity of the Art itself.

Personally, I enjoy Tae Kwon Do, but there are several other types disciplines such as, Karate, Aikido, Jujitsu, Kung Fu, etc. Visit them and find the one that interest you and the studio team that you fit best with. Not every studio is for every person, so find the one that is best for you. The studio staff, the students and the instructors will become a family of sorts to you, and you will gain a whole other network of people you can count on and trust.

Don't be afraid to ask questions and really understand what is going to be taught and how it will be taught. Remember even though the person you are talking with may be a high level instructor, or when you walked in, you see all these people doing things that look like Bruce Lee, they all started just like you. Every one of them looked clumsy and silly when they started, but with time and effort they have progressed and so will you.

If you are looking for just some self-defense tactics, there are a lot of self-defense classes, and even schools. Some of the Martial Arts Academies will teach self-defense as part of their curriculum. The key to finding a good place to learn, is to use your brain and your heart. I will repeat myself here. Talk with the instructor and staff, tour the studio, and if you are comfortable with the people and the environment, trust that and go forth. If not, trust that and look for another place to learn. But keep in mind, you should have a little apprehension or fear, that is natural when doing something new.

Take a Self-Defense Class

A good self-defense class is the best way to protect yourself from an attacker. The chapter in this book on tactics, gives you some quick and basic moves that can help to defend yourself,

TIP

Second Nature

When something no longer requires energy to think about, You simply just do it.

but good self-defense can only be taught in person. You need to have a trained instructor walking you through the moves so you get them correct. Getting the moves correct is important, so you do not hurt yourself and are most effective when executing the move. Then you need to practice the moves, so they become second nature.

A good self-defense class, will teach you many things, not just how to punch and kick the attacker. The instructor will teach you how to size up a situation, so you can decide the best course of action. In an good self-defense class, you will learn how to catch the attacker off guard and surprise the attacker. You will learn how to regain control of the situation, so you are in charge not the attacker. A good self-defense instructor, will teach you special techniques to break the grip of an attacker and other ways for you to get away.

On top of all of the cool techniques you will learn, in a good self-defense class, you will learn one very important thing. You will learn self-confidence. During the self-defense class, you will practice the techniques so many times, they will become a natural reaction.

You will become so confident in your ability, that when the situation arises, you will not think, you will simply react.

During the self-defense class, you will practice the techniques several times. If you take a self-defense class with a friend you can practice after the class is over, to keep your skills sharp. This will help you to keep the moves fresh in your mind and in the memory of your muscles, so they are ready to be used if you need them.

Chapter 9 ➤

Techniques
(Not intended to replace training)

> *"The Last Resort is to physically stop the threat."*

I can never emphasize enough, that the best self-defense, is being prepared. A large part of being prepared for self-defense, is training. Earlier we talked about taking a self-defense class, and I gave you some pointers on choosing an appropriate class for yourself. With that in mind, DO NOT assume that the techniques I am about to explain are in any way intended to replace proper training. These techniques are simple gross motor skill movements, that we all naturally do, we are just going to talk about targeting them towards an attacker.

By knowing a few basic self-defense moves, you could save your life or the life of someone else. The moves we are going to be talking about, anyone can do, regardless of age, shape or size. A good defense is practice, when an attack happens, it happens fast. We do not have time to decide what to do, we only have time to react. Therefore it is important to practice the moves, so they become second nature and become engrained in your muscle memory.

The only rule to fighting an attacker is that there are no rules, anything goes, your job is to get away alive.

The best self-defense, is prevention. Bad guys are looking for an easy target. Being prepared and paying attention makes you a hard target and the bad guys will look for a target that is easier and leave you alone. Sometimes though, the villain attacks no matter what we do, this is where the preparation pays off and your skills will keep you alive.

If you are confronted or attacked, try to defuse the situation by talking to the bad guy. Every situation is different, throughout this book I have given you some tips and techniques to help you deal with the situation.

It will be up to you, to try different ones, that you feel best fit the situation at hand. The most valuable thing you possess is your life, nothing else is worth more than that, so if the criminal is demanding your keys, wallet, jewelry, etc. give it to them. Tossing the items off to the side, is a good way in which to cause a distraction, that may buy you just enough time to get away.

I have said it several times already, and will probably say it several more times before this book is complete. Get away if and when you can. There is no need to stay and fight. Be smart and get away, run, scream, make a lot of noise and run away. However, it may not always be possible to get away, and fighting may be your only option. If this is the case, then the only other option is to fight to stay alive, stay calm and you will survive.

Kick to the groin
The kick to the groin has been a long time favorite, we have taught it to our children, our parents taught us, their parents taught them all the way back to the beginning of history. Just to be sure we all understand

where we are talking about, the groin is the place below the belly button where the legs come together. Also known as between the legs. We have always been told that when a male attacker  comes at you to kick him in the groin, it is an effective and a simple move, but don't forget it also works when a female comes at you. Female attackers are not expecting to be kicked in the groin, so it catches them off guard and it still hurts, giving you time to get away.

When kicking to the groin use your knee if you can, as your knee is harder and you will not have to extend your leg out there for the bad guy to catch it. Also keep in mind that when striking with your knee to use the top part of the knee (actually it is more like the very end of your femur right where the knee starts to bend). The knee cap is very fragile and striking with it will hurt you more than it will the bad guy. Whenever you are kicking try to hit the person with a boney part of your leg like your shin. This will hurt them more.

Remember the point here, is to inflict as much pain on the other person as possible.

Fingers

Your fingers can be a great weapon. Have you ever had a cat claw you, think of your fingers like cat claws. You can jab your fingers (claws) into the attackers forehead and drag down their face, fast and hard. I know it sounds mean, but remember the person is attacking you and your only objective is to get away alive.

Eyes

Eyes are a nice soft spot to hurt the attacker, you can poke, gouge, scratch, put your fingers in them, use your knuckles. This will hurt the bad guy as well it will also interfere with their vision, and give you a chance to get away.

Use your thumbs to push hard on the persons eyes, push so hard that you could push their eyes into their head. Yes it is going to hurt, that is the idea, hurt the bad guy so they don't hurt you.

Throat / Neck

The throat is a vulnerable place on an attacker, use your hands, fists, elbows, or anything else you have to strike the attacker in the throat. Hit the bad guy as hard as you can, it will hurt them and they will probably lose their breath for a moment.

The neck is home to major arteries and a group of nerves called the brachial plexus. Which is a network of nerves connecting the spine to the arm. It is located right above the collar bone on both sides of the neck. A sharp hard strike to this area will stun the bad guy, making his arm useless for a short time, giving you time to get away.

Stomp on their foot

If the bad guy has you in a bear hug, or has grabbed you form behind, you can stomp on their foot. Raise your foot up and as you stomp down as hard as you can, scrape your foot along their shin causing more pain. Try to land your stomp, on the little bones on top of the foot where the foot joins the ankle (instep), you will have a good chance of breaking their foot at this point. Put as much weight as you can on the heel of your foot as you stomp and grind it into the top of the criminals foot. While you are still standing on their foot, push them away from you. If you hold their foot in place when they fall, their ankle will break and you can now get away.

Ears

The ears are a great place to slap, pull, bite, whatever you can do that causes pain. By cupping your hands like you are trying to hold water and slapping the ears, you cause a lot of pain and temporarily cause the person to not be able to hear.

Head But

If the bad guys has a grip on you from behind, you can throw your head back into their forehead, nose or face. Yes this is going to hurt you some as well, but it will hurt them a whole lot more, and will stun them just enough to give you a small amount of time to get away.

Voice

We all have our own personal space, as soon as someone invades your personal space, or makes you feel uncomfortable, let them and everyone around you know it by yelling. "Back off", "Stop" are great commands, they will get the attention of the bad guy as well as anyone else who can hear you. This also lets the villain know that you are not an easy target, there is a good chance they will move on at this point, because you are too much trouble for them.

Shouting or screaming with each strike does a couple of things. It catches the attacker off guard, remember they want an easy target. It tightens up your core (stomach area), allowing you to generate more power. It ensures you are breathing, believe it or not many people forget to breath when they are in a fight situation. This is bad, as you can pass out, when you do not breath, so breath.

One of the most important things, shouting and yelling does, is it alerts others to your situation. They can now come to help, call police, be a witness, or anything else they choose, but at least you are not alone now.

Nose

We have all been hit in the nose, and we all know it hurts. So use this to your advantage, strike the attacker with the palm of your hand with an upward blow to the nose. Use your elbow to smash the attacker in the nose. Use your forehead to smash their nose. Cause as much pain as you can.

Knee

A strong kick to the side of the bad guys knee will knock them off balance, and if hard enough, will break his knee, giving you time to get away.

Push

This is a simple move but it takes courage sometimes to execute it. When the bad guy comes up and challenges you, take both of your hands, using the palms of your hands push the bad guy on their chest as hard as you can. Shove the villain back and continue a couple of times. Many times this is all it takes, and the attacker will back off. They are looking for the easy target and by pushing back you are showing them that you will not take it from them. Oh and don't forget to yell and scream.

This is also one of those times when you need to make a situational decision. Pushing the bad guy could also set them off, and now they become more aggressive. So use your best judgment, to decide if this is a good tactic to use at this point in the game.

Stances

Staying light on your feet will give you the advantage in a dangerous situation. You need to have your feet well positioned. If you do not you, could fall over easily. Stay light on your feet, ready to move any direction you need to.

Ready Stance

Standing in a comfortable position, with your feet shoulder width apart, with your hands open about chest level. Keeping your eyes on the other person and looking at their chest, this way you can see any movement of their body whether it be their hands, feet or legs. Keep the other person out of your personal zone, at least 4 feet away and out of arms reach. This way you have a little more time, to react, if they make a move. With your hands in this open position at chest level, it is a non-threatening motion, yet it allows you the opportunity to quickly protect your head or body if you need to.

Defensive Stance

Step back with your dominate shoulder and leg back. Stepping back allows you to create a little more space between you and the bad guy. By putting your dominate side back, you are positioning yourself to generate more power with your best kicking and punching side. Tuck your chin down, bringing your hands up alongside your face to protect your face and jaw. Tuck your elbows in to protect your ribs. Your feet should be shoulder width apart and your knees slightly bent. You should be up on the balls of your feet, ready to move any direction you need to. If you could see yourself in the mirror, you would look like a boxer, ready to knock out your opponent.

Stepping off line

When a person attacks us, they tend to come straight at us, by simply stepping to one side or the other, we can avoid their attack. This is called stepping off line, you can step, jump, slid, whatever it takes to get out of the path, of the attacker. By stepping off line, you have taken the power out of the attack. Now the bad guy is going to regroup rather quickly and try again. When you step off line, be prepared to deliver some kind of attack (or rather defensive move) on the bad guy. Throwing several punches, kick and knees are all great things, just be sure to try and get three or more strikes in if you can. Just as always, if you get the chance to get away, that is the best you can do, run.

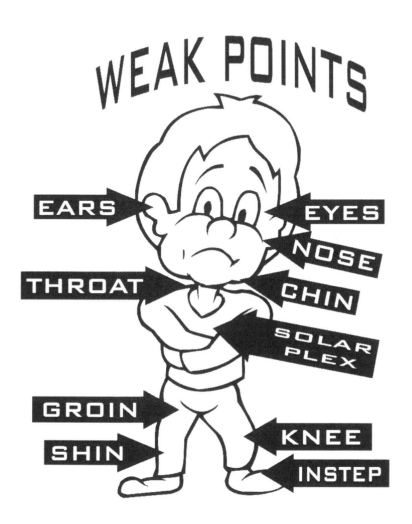

Chapter 10 ➡️

The secret to my success

"What is the secret to your success in life?"

People are always asking me, what is the secret to your success in life? To tell you the truth, it took me a while to put my finger on it. Maybe, I am just not as bright as I think I am. Because, now that I truly understand it, it seems like a no brainer.

Secrets are usually meant to be guarded and kept to yourself, but I am going to let you in on my secret. Well do not let me lie to you, it really is not a secret. You see, the reason my life has gone the way it has to this point, and why I have enjoyed to the blessings in my life which I have, is all because of the relationship I have with a very good friend of mine.

I spent the early part of my life, up until I was 21 with my friend being far off, and not really inviting Him into my life much. Even though I did not ask Him to be around, or take part in my life, He was always there, watching me from the distance and making sure I did not stray too far way. Then through some common friends, I started hanging out with my friend a lot more, and inviting Him to join me and my friends, in our day to day activities. Ever since then, I have enjoyed a blessed life. Do not get me wrong, not a life free of troubles. But, the troubles I have, I know I can handle them, because I have good friends to stand by me.

You probably know my good friend, because He is in your life as well. His name is Jesus Christ. Hopefully you are a bit brighter than I am, and you invite Him to hang out with you in your life. If you have not yet, I encourage you to do so, He will bless your life more than you could ever imagine.

Over the years I have learned some pretty cool things, and I have seen some even more amazing things. Things that only through Jesus Christ could they transpire. They say, that faith is believing in things that are not seen. I can honestly say that I have never seen Jesus. Except for in an dream, hanging on a cross with two others, hanging on crosses next to Him, on top of a small hill. (The only reason this is significant to me, is because I do not remember any of my dreams except this one). Even though I have never seen Jesus on Earth, I know with an unshakable knowledge that He is The Christ, He atoned for my sins, as well as your sins, He paid the price of freedom for all of us to enjoy, if we but follow him.

I can also testify to you, that our Heavenly Father loves us so much that he sent His only begotten Son to Earth, knowing full well that the people of Earth, His children, Jesus' siblings, would kill Him. Heavenly Father did this because He knew, that this is the way it needed to be, so that we all can again live with him for Eternity. But, there is a condition to that, we must accept this plan and what Christ has done for us, and follow His commandments, thereby freeing us from the bondage of evil.

The best part of this is, we do not have to do this alone. We have each other to use as support as we struggle through life. We have the Scriptures to guide us, and the best part is the Lord has given us living Prophets to guide us in these latter days.

To answer the question – "What is the secret to my success in life?" It is simple, I keep my friend Jesus Christ first in my Life!

Social self-defense is more of a total picture of self-defense. It encompasses not only the physical act of defending one-self, but also *a change in mind* where we become aware of our surroundings and thereby create a safe zone where we are less likely to become a victim. Social self-defense is doing everything possible to AVOID fighting the attacker. Social self-defense is all about using the gray squishy stuff between your ears, and **being smarter than the bad guy.**

Info@socialself-defense.com
WWW.SOCIALSELF-DEFENSE.COM

ADD-ON PROGRAM
Many self-defense or martial arts schools are already providing great training in the physical portion of self-defense.

Our programs are the natural supplementation to the physical training. Adding Social Self-defense to your existing program will enhance your program, adding value and desirability.

To schedule speakers, seminars, and trainings, visit our website.

Order books, items and more, from our website.

PRESENTATIONS
If a more hands on approach is desired, Social Self-defense will come to your location and deliver an informative and exciting seminar in conjunction with a hands on interactive training session.

17108918R00060

Made in the USA
Charleston, SC
27 January 2013